Maintaining
"The Presence"

by Kevin J. Conner

Published by Conner Ministries Ltd

WEB: kevinconner.org
Email: kevin.conner321@gmail.com

Visit www.amazon.com/author/kevinjconner for a list of
other books by Kevin Conner.

Table of Contents

Maintaining "The Presence"

Introductory:
A Great Bible Theme, overlooked by so many preachers and teachers is that which concerns "The Presence".

Just a glance at the references to this great theme in Strong's Concordance shows the importance of this great theme. This is what this Booklet is about. It shows the necessity of maintaining The Presence of the Lord, both, in a Christians' personal life and in Church Life.

Otherwise all, especially in Church Life, all can become an empty and lifeless formalism.

Read on and be challenged and changed- and if need be - convicted - if you and your Church Life has drifted into an empty, religious formalism. This Booklet is written more specifically to Ministers of the Gospel, and to all preachers and teachers of the timeless truths of the Word of God.

Kevin J. Conner
Melbourne, Australia
2015-16

CHAPTER ONE

Some Sample Scriptures on "The Presence"

There are many sample Scriptures on the Presence of God, some of which are noted here.

1. Adam & Eve - the moment sin entered the world, hid themselves from the presence of the Lord - Gen.3:8
2. Cain went out from the presence of the Lord to dwelt in the land of Nod, after he killed his brother Abel and his rejection of the lamb - Gen.4:1-16
3. Moses said to the Lord as God spoke with him. "My **Presence** shall go with you and I will give you rest...if Your **Presence** goes not with me...carry us not hence... Read the whole passage - Ex.33:10-23. Moses valued the Presence of the Lord for the journey.
4. One of the warnings to the wicked in Israel was that they would be "cut off from the Presence of the Lord" Lev 22:3.
5. King David valued the Presence of the Lord. This is seen in the following Psalms, with the emphasis on the **Presence** of the Lord - the reader is encouraged to note these Scriptures from the Psalms. Here are some brief quotes:
   - Psa.9:3, 11
   - Psa.17:2
   - Psa.51:11. Cast me not away from Your Presence
   - Psa.97:5
   - Psa.100:2. Come before His Presence with singing
   - Psa114:7
   - Psa. 116:14, 18

Isaiah the Prophet

- Isa.64:1-3. The mountains flow down at His Presence
- The angel Gabriel - he stood in the Presence of the Lord, waiting for the Word of His command.
- Peter - Times of refreshing will come from the Presence of the Lord - Acts 3:19.
  It literally means "The Face that toward or away."
  Read also - Dt.31:17-18; 33:20; Psa.13:1; 27:9; Ezek.39:29; Mic.3:4 and Hos.5:15.
  These references taken from KJV. Refer also for others in Strong's Concordance.

A brief reading of these Scriptures showed how some of the saints really valued His Presence, and what it meant to them .

CHAPTER TWO

ASPECTS OF HIS PRESENCE

There are two major aspects of "The Presence of the Lord" as taught in the Scriptures and as we understand. These are Omnipresence and what could be spoken of Localized Presence.

1. Omnipresence
    These are qualities of God that make God who He is. No creature or created being has these qualities.
    *   Omniscient - God knows all things and all creatures at all times. There is nothing any creature can tell Him that He does not already know. This is beyond human comprehension.
    *   Omnipotent
        God is all powerful. He has and controls the universe of planets, including both heaven and earth. There is nothing He cannot do.
    *   Omnipresent
        God is everywhere present at all times. God does not or cannot go anywhere. He is already there. He is omnipresent, and He is everywhere at all times.

Such a Being, creatures, neither angels or mankind, cannot comprehend with our finite minds. We accept the Biblical revelation in faith, and wonder and worship.

Jesus as the God-Man put it this way, because of who He was and is, "Where two or three are gathered together, in My

Name, there I AM in the midst of them." Note Matt.18:20 with the Amplified N.T.

He also said, "Lo, I AM with you unto the end of this world 16(this age)...Go and make disciples of all nations." - Matt.28:16-20.

Surely this is omnipresence, omnipotence and omniscience! And that of the Lord Jesus Himself as the God-Man, God incarnate.

2. Localized Presence
   Although God is omnipotent, everywhere at all times, displaying at all times, His attributes that make God, God, He has been pleased to, what may be called, to manifest His "localized Presence."

   This is particularly in relation to and for His people. Several examples of this are seen in the following illustrations and are set forth as examples of His "Localized Presence" and this is what this Booklet is about!

   - The Pillar of the Cloud that lead Israel to the Promised Land - Ex.14:19-24

   - God appearing to Moses in the Burning Bush. From here God called Moses to deliver His people Israel from the bondages of Egyptian task-masters - Ex.3

   - God appeared between the Cherubim on the Ark of the Covenant. He spoke audibly to Aaron as High Priest, or Moses, as the Law-giver, from time to time. This was from the blood-stained mercy-seat - Read Ex.37:1-9 with Num.7:89.

- Even though there may be controversy and differing opinions, the Star in the East was possibly the Shekinah Glory that lead the Wise Men to the Christ-child (not forbidden Magicians) - Num.24:17 with Matt.2

- The Angel of His Presence - Isa.63:8-10. KJV. This was possibly the Lord Jesus Christ in Theophanic form (or what is called a Christ-ophany).
The Scripture is so explicit that this was no ordinary "Angel." The Scripture reads: "For He said, Surely they are My people, children that will not lie; so He was their Saviour. In all their affliction, He was afflicted, and the Angel (Messenger) of **His Presence** saved them: in His love and in His pity He redeemed them; and he bare them and carried them all the days of old."

Even though all readers may not accept these things, yet there is enough evidence in Scripture where the "Localized Presence" was manifested in, amongst and for, the people (the OT Israel) of God.

This is what is meant by the "Localized Presence" of God.

7

CHAPTER THREE

ORDINANCES OR RITUALS?

All God-given ordinances or anything given by Christ can become Ritualism if we do not maintain "The Presence" in any or each of them. But let us define what is meant by these words. What is the difference between an ordinance and a ritual?

Depending on the Dictionary used, the words take on significant meaning.

1. Ordinances
    From the American Dictionary of the English language, we have a condensed meaning of the word "Ordinances."
    "A rule established by an authority; a permanent rule of action. In this sense, it is often used in Scripture (Ex.15; Num.10; Ezra 3). It is an observance, or an appointment. In this sense, Baptism and the Lord's Supper are denominated as *ordinances.*

2. Ritualism
    From Collins Dictionary we get the word "rite" (ritualism, ritualistic, etc).
    The **rite** and related words are defined as "a custom, or a formal act of religion or usage." One can become ritualistic and miss the spirit of the ordinance. In other words, one can slip from the ordinance into ritualism where, even ordinances ordained of God, or of Christ, can become a mere form, a ritual, because there is no Presence in it. That's what we are talking about! This will be seen more fully in the following chapters. The Lord Jesus ordained some ordinances in Church

Life and all can become a lifeless form, a mere custom without "the Presence" there.

We, as Minister's, must maintain "The Presence" in each and every ordinance established in Church Life. That is the real issue!

CHAPTER FOUR

THE LORD'S TABLE - COMMUNION

The writer in his early Christian days once belonged to a Denomination, where I had to come call myself "an unbelieving believer." In this Denomination we did not believe in the Lord's Table, or even Water Baptism, and a host of other Biblical ordinances.

In due time, through the Lord's leading, this writer found himself in a Pentecostal Church where they believe in the Lord's Table and in Water Baptism. They practised this ordinance each Sunday.

From time to time, the Minister would say, "We are going to partake of Communion, or the Lord's Supper. There is nothing in the bread, nothing in the cup, but let's look away to the Lord!"

One can only read what went on in my mind. "Nothing in the bread, and nothing in the cup." So the writer would think this way (though not say anything), "Lord, bless this "nothing; may we get "nothing" out of it." Most got "nothing" out of it. It just became a ritual, a memorial service, a mere form, even though the Lord had ordained it.

Later on, it was seen that Paul explained that "many were sick and feeble and even some died" for not discerning the Lord's Body, the Body of Christ in the Communion (1Cor.11:23-34). One can eat bread and drink the cup all day and not get sick or weakly or die. There must be something in it!

Many found they were physically healed and strengthened. There was impartation of life in discerning the Lord's body and blood of the Lord Jesus Christ, What was it? "The Presence."

Otherwise, the very thing that the Lord ordained can become a Church Ritual, without His Presence. In the Old Testament, the Table of Showbread was called (Marginal reading), "The Bread of His Presence" or "Presence Bread." Read Num.4:7; 1Sam.21:6; Ex.25:30 with Ex.35:13; 39:36. See NASB Translation - 1963.

Anything can become a Church Ritual, a lifeless form, if we do not maintain "the Presence." overshadowing the Table, even though the Head of the Church, the Lord Jesus ordained it. It becomes a dead and lifeless ritual without "the Presence."

CHAPTER FIVE

THE ANOINTING OIL

Jesus sent out the Twelve as they preached the Gospel of the Kingdom. We read in Mark's Gospel that they anointed many that were sick and they were healed - Mrk.6:1-13.

In Church Life, if any were sick, they could call the elders of the Church and they would anoint them with oil. The elders could pay over them, anoint them with oil. If there was sin in their lives, then confession would take place. The Lord would heal and raise them up - Jas.5:13-16.

What was the secret? Maintaining "the Presence." An example may be seen in 1Sam.15:33. Oil is the symbol of the Holy Spirit. It is like, on this occasion, that the Holy Spirit is saying, "that anointing oil is the symbol of My own Being, and I work with the symbol of My Being." The Holy Spirit came upon David from that day forward.

The Holy Spirit worked with the symbol of His own Being. He was "The Presence." When the anointing oil touched David, THE HOLY SPIRIT also touched David. THE anointing came when the anointing oil touched him.

When we, as elders in Church Life, anoint the sick with oil, do we have any expectation? Could we expect THE Holy Spirit to work with the symbol of His own Being? Could we expect THE Holy Spirit - THE Holy Oil - to come on folks from that day forward?

Otherwise, as has been said, it becomes a dead and lifeless ritual and formalism creeps in. The Holy Spirit is "the Presence" once again.

Let us make way for the Holy Spirit to come and not degenerate into empty and lifeless ritualism. He works with the symbol of His own Being! Make room for Him as "the Presence."

CHAPTER SIX

THE LAYING ON OF HANDS

Jesus said, as part of His commission, "They shall lay hands of the sick and they shall recover." Mrk.16:15-18.

In the Book of Acts, they laid hands on people and the sick were healed - Read Acts 5:12; 8:7-8; 9:4, 17; 14:8-9; 19:12-13; 19:11-12.

The Book of Acts also tells how the Baptism of the Holy Spirit was imparted and people spoke with new tongues as the Spirit gave them the utterance - Acts 19:1-6 with Acts 2:4. It was not a matter of "laying empty hands on empty heads." There was "the Presence."

Simon wanted the power to lay hands on people for the Baptism of the Holy Spirit - Acts 8:17-19. He must have seen and heard something.

There was an impartation in the laying on of hands. There was "the Presence" in the laying on of hands. It was not a form or ritual. There was power there. It was simply the Presence of the Lord. This is what the leader should expect!

CHAPTER SEVEN

THE ORDINANCE OF WATER BAPTISM

Jesus, as the Builder of His Church, also gave the ordinance of Water Baptism. "He that believes and is baptized shall be saved" - Mrk.16:15-18.

He commanded in Matthews 28:18-20 His disciples to go into all the world and make disciples of all nations as they preached the Gospel of the Kingdom. They were to immerse believers in (into. Grk) the Name of the Father, and of the Son and of the Holy Spirit.

In Mark 16:15-18 this ordinance was only for believers, otherwise one goes down into the water a dry sinner and comes up a wet one!

In Acts on the Day of Pentecost, the birthday of the Church, Peter, the leading apostle commanded Water Baptism in the Name of the Lord Jesus Christ, which is THE NAME of the Father, Son and Holy Spirit. Refer Acts 2:37-47.

In the earliest MSS water baptism was simply in (into) the Name of the Lord Jesus Christ, The Church, in general over the years degenerated and this ordinance fell into the "Doctrine of Baptismal Regeneration" Whereby a person is "born again." This comes by a misunderstanding and misinterpreting of this wonderful ordinance - Read and understand John 3:1-12 with Mark 16:15-18 and Gal.3:27-28.

Some Ministers of the Gospel, in reaction to this falsity of teaching in Water Baptism, often state, "there's nothing in the water; it is just an outward sign of an inward experience."

15

Over the years of understanding of the Word, this writer came to see that the FIRST of **water and the Spirit,** was found in Gen.1:1-2. It says there that "**the Spirit of God moved (hovered) over the face of the waters."**

Remember this writer did not originally believe in Water Baptism. As he studied this Scripture, the Scripture opened up. This was the real secret of the ordinance of Water Baptism. This was the key. This was "the Presence." The Spirit moved on the water.

The end result was there came out of darkness, light. There came order from chaos, and fruitfulness from barrenness. This was "the Presence" of the Holy Spirit of God moving on the face of the water!

The question could be asked: Could the Spirit move - "the Presence" - ,move on the face of the water in Water Baptism so that the candidate indeed would "rise to walk in newness of life?" The answer is "Yes!"

Paul interprets Water Baptism in Rom.6:1-6 and Gal.3:27 as into the death, burial and resurrection of Christ, and the putting on of Christ.

This writer believes so. This is done by maintaining "the Presence" of the Holy Spirit, moving on the face of the waters so that the candidate does rise to walk in the new life in Christ. If folks have been bound by drugs or other life-threatening habits, they can indeed come out of such by the power of the Spirit as in Gen.1:1-2. This could (should) as we maintain "the Presence" in this wonderful ordinance.

CHAPTER EIGHT

THE MINISTRY OF THE WORD

Paul exhorted his son in the faith and in the Lord to spread the Word. He told him to "Preach the Word, be instant in season, out of season..." - 2Tim.4:2 & 2Tim. 3:14-17.

Any Preacher or Teacher of the Word, in honesty, can speak of times when the principle of which we speak, there was no "Presence" when speaking. There was no quickening, no touch of the Holy Spirit. It seemed as if the speaker was just multiplying words, mind to mind having no real communication or that mysterious touch of the Spirit. There was no touch of the "Presence" while speaking. The Preacher knew it and some of the people knew it.

It has been said that all preaching/teaching should involve mind, emotions and will.

1. The Mind - inform the mind; intelligent communication to the mind, not merely a mind to mind battle
2. The Emotions - stir the emotions, not merely emotionalism
3. The Will - move the will to respond to the will of the Word of God.

We see this preaching power on the Day of Pentecost when Peter spoke the Word. Some 3000 souls responded to that convicting Word and were added to the Church.

The mind was informed, by the Word. The emotions were stirred and people responded willingly to that Word - Acts 2. During Church History there have sporadic waves of this kind

Of Ministry of the Word (Read of some of these 'Revivals' which came upon the Church at various periods of time).

What was it, again we ask? It was that mysterious Presence of the Holy Spirit, touching lives; mentally, emotionally and volitionally: that is; mind, emotions and will.

If it is of the mind only, then it is only mind to mind, communication only.
If it is of the emotions only, then it could be merely emotionalism.
If it of the will only, then it may only be self-will.

But if "the Presence" is there, then it may just be of the Holy Spirit, convicting souls of their need of Jesus as Lord and their Saviour.

As Preachers and Teachers of the Word of God, seek the Lord for "the Presence". There can be far more lasting results. That's what we are talking about!

CHAPTER NINE

THE HEM OF HIS GARMENT

Jesus was always "a carrier of God's Presence." Where ever He went there was always "The Presence" of God there, so much so, virtue or healing power went out of Him.

People touched the hem of His garments and the people were healed - for examples - read Mrk.5:25-38; Matt.9:20-22; 14:36.

Upon the hem of the garments the High Priest wore, there was a golden bell and a pomegranate (gifts & fruits), so his sound could be heard as he moved in the Sanctuary - Ex.39:24-26.

Jesus was moved with compassion as He healed the sick and The suffering people in His times - Mrk.1:41; 5:19; 6:34; 9:22; Lke.7:13; 10:33; Matt.20:34.

Jesus is our High Priest, after the order of Melchizedek and as sick people touched the HEM of His garment, they were healed. What was it, may be asked again? Simply "the Presence", by the power of the Holy Spirit and His Divine compassion.

The same is true of people in the time of Paul. God worked Special and unusual miracles by the hands of Paul. Even handkerchiefs and aprons were taken from Paul's body and the diseases left and even demon spirits departed from people who were inflicted by such - Read Acts 19:11-13.

What was the secret? "The Presence" of the Lord, not the power in the handkerchiefs or aprons! One could lay such all over people and none would be healed. It was that mysterious

19

"Presence", the power of the Holy Spirit at work again.

Otherwise, it could be made a rite, or a custom and no one would get healed or evil spirits leave them.

Paul, like Jesus, like Peter, were "***carriers of the Presence***" - This was the key!

CHAPTER TEN

THE POWERLESS NAME

Following on from the unusual miracles, we have this account given in the Book of Acts - Acts 19:13-20.

There we have the seven sons of Sceva, sons of a Jewish priest, trying to cast out evil spirits in the Name of Jesus whom Paul preached. What was the response?

The man in whom the evil spirit was, said "Jesus I know, Paul I know, but who are you?" The man in whom was the evil spirit, leaped on them, overpowered them and prevailed. They fled out of the house naked and wounded.

The end results were good. Fear fell on the Greeks. The Name of Jesus was magnified. Many of the believers came confessing, burning their magic books, which summed up in total 50,000 silver pieces. The Word of the Lord grew and prevailed.

The Name of Jesus was powerless on the lips of these seven sons of Sceva, sons of a vagabond Jewish priest. It was a powerless Name. Why?

There are a number of lessons that one may learn from this account in the Book of Acts. Any leader, Preacher/Teacher or believers may learn from this account. Let us note the number of them:

- They were religious people
- They were sons of a high priest
- They had no personal relationship with the Lord Jesus

21

- They used Jesus' Name as they used a magic word
- The evil spirit in the man knew Jesus and Paul, but not the sons of this ex-priest
- The Name of Jesus was powerless on their lips
- There was no "Presence"" there and the Name of Jesus was powerless on their lips
- The demon spirits knew it but these sons of Sceva did not know it.

There are plenty of lessons for all to learn. There was not the personal, living, relationship with the Lord Jesus Christ. Jesus said, "Whatever you ask the Father in MY NAME He will do it for you" - NOTE especially John 16:23-24- Amp. NT.

The seven sons of Sceva had no personal relationship with the Father, to ask the Father, in His Name - presenting all I AM - to cast out these evil spirits. No wonder they fled the house naked and ashamed! The Name of Jesus was just used as an empty, powerless, magic word, on their lips.

It is "the Presence" that gives power to His Name. This comes about by a personal relationship with the Person whose Name it is! Otherwise "The Name" is powerless on our lips.

CHAPTER ELEVEN

THE SHADOW OF PETER

At various times, the Lord did some unusual acts - Read Isa.28:21. Here it speaks of God's "strange work; His strange act."

In the Book of Acts we see some of God's "strange acts". This time in relation to the apostle Peter - Acts 5:14-17. We quote the passage.

"And believers were increasingly added to the Lord, multitudes of both men and women, so that they brought the sick into the streets and laid them on beds and couches, that at least the shadow of Peter passing by might fall on them.
Also a multitude gathered from the surrounding cities to Jerusalem bringing sick people and those who were tormented by unclean spirits, and they were all healed."

Certainly an unusual act, a strange act of the Lord. They were all healed. The shadow of Peter bringing healing to sick people and unclean spirits delivering people.

As the Scripture say, they were ALL healed, made whole. The healing and delivering power of the Lord was there. What was it? In other words, as noted in various cases, it was "the Presence" - the Presence of the Lord, the localized Presence of the Lord Jesus Christ Himself, ministering through and by the shadow of Peter.

One could walk by people all day and every day, and cast shadows here and there, but it was "the Presence" of the Lord who made the difference.

23

As has been noted before, Peter, as Jesus, as Paul were the carriers of "the Presence" as they went here and there.

There is no other account of this, but it did happen as the Presence of the Lord was here. It could happen again if God willed to do His "strange work, His strange act."

This also shows that the faith of the people was on a high level when this happened. It was not just Peter's shadow, but it was "the Presence" of the healing Christ.

CHAPTER TWELVE

WORSHIP SERVICES AND MEETINGS

As we bring our study to a close, we look at regular worship services and finally one OT picture of Localized Presence.

Without doubt, the greatest passage in the Bible on the subject of "Worship" is John 4:20-24 linked with Matthew 18:20. The guarantee of "the Presence" is the latter verse where Jesus Himself said, "Where two or three are gathered together in (into) My Name, there I AM in the midst of them." (Amp. NT).

The Greek thought is where two or three gather together, and one as a whole, and there make an orchestral sound (symphonize, make a harmony) in My Name, there I am in the middle of them. It is the guarantee of the "Presence."

God is a Spirit and true worship must be "in spirit" and "in truth." True worship comes from our spirit to God who is Spirit.

Our worship to be "in spirit" and "in truth" must be from our spirit and in harmony with the Word of God, the Word of Truth - Jhn.17:17

Many years ago, some folks remarked to me that "they did not get anything out of the worship". Responding to this, my remarks were, "You did not get anything out of the worship? Did GOD get anything out of it; after all who is worship for any way?"

There are songs/hymns/choruses that we humans really enjoy and give enthusiastic clapping give of them. . And there are songs/hymns/choruses that the Holy Spirit confirms in a specific way - "the Presence" - where He really enjoys and there is that touch of the Spirit on songs which exalt the Lord Jesus Christ. There is a place for both groupings/

Great responsibility is on the Song or Worship leader in choosing songs (etc) that lead the people to truly worship the Father in spirit and in truth. It means understanding what constitute "praise" songs and "worship" songs. Some folks - Churches - major on "praise" and some on "worship" songs. Praise is an emphasis on **what God has done** and worship is an emphasis on **WHO God is!** Praise should lead into worship!

It is sadly possible to become a "Laodicean Church", and be singing songs so loud that He is outside and we cannot hear His gentle knocking to come into the service. He is outside His own Church, while they are "worshipping" in the service!

It is sadly possible to become lukewarm, and have "devotion in motion this side of the ocean" - as has been said - and not be hot nor cold. This can make Christ sick.

He wants us to open the door, allow Him - "the Presence" - to enter into the service. The principle is the parents of Jesus **supposed** He was with them and they sought Him sorrowing for several days until they found Him the Temple, His Father's house and business - Rev. 3:14-22 with Lke.2:41-50.

By His Holy Spirit He is "the Presence."

CHAPTER THIRTEEN

THE ARK OF THE COVENANT

As noted, this is the final chapter. It is an illustration from the Old Testament.

The most important article of furniture in the Tabernacle of Moses was the Ark of the Covenant. All the other articles were affected and took value from the Ark of the Covenant. Why?

Because the very Shekinah Glory Presence was on the Ark of God. For Israel, this was the "localized Presence" of God in His Tabernacle. There, between the Cherubim was the Glory of God. The voice of God actually spoke to the High Priest from time to time from off the blood-stained Mercy Seat. There was "the Presence." It was Himself who spoke to the High Priest. This was the localized Presence of God in Israel, dwelling in their midst. God was with them in that Cloud of Glory.

The Glory-Cloud governed their movements. When the Cloud lifted, they moved on. When the Cloud remained, they remained. All eyes were on that Glory-Cloud for their movements - Read Ex.25:10-22 with Ex.40:34-38/

BUT there came a time in Israel where the people took it for granted and the Ark became a kind of superstition. "The Presence" had gone.

When the time came that Israel was pressed by the Philistines, they decided that, superstitiously, they would bring the Ark of God from Shiloh. When the Ark of God came, they shouted, but it was an empty shout. Long-story-short: The Ark of God was taken captive, Eli died, Phinehas and Hophni died, and a child was born, named **Ichabod** - The glory has departed. For details of this the reader is encouraged to read Deut.10:8; 1Sam.4:1-22; 6:3; 1Chron.15:2.

Instead of referring the Glory Cloud and the localized "Presence" they referred to the Ark of God as **"it"**- NKJV, 1Sam.4:3. It was no longer "HIM" but an "IT" because the Glory had departed. There was no longer "the Presence."

The Ark was no longer that which was **personal** but it became **Impersonal.!**

Such can happen in a Church. All these religious, life-giving ordinances can become ritualistic and lifeless. They can be an "it" because there is no personal relationship with the Lord by the Spirit, who is the **Living Presence!**

This is what this Booklet is about; not to let Jesus-ordained ordinances to become lifeless rituals or forms.

CONCLUSION

Our study is completed. The conclusion concerns lessons that are re-iterated throughout these chapters. These lessons learnt become a fitting conclusion to our studies.

1. Make room for the Holy Spirit, "the Presence" at the beginning of service, not at end, as merely the Benediction. That is the wrong end of the meeting as people are leaving.

2. Beware of the dangers of ritualism and formalism when conducting any of Jesus' ordinances, the things He has established in Church Life.

3. Maintain "the Presence" by daily relationship that comes by seeking the face of the Lord.

4. Beware of Magic, Romanism or Pentecostal witchcraft

5. Remember the Holy Spirit is "the Presence" of the Lord in the Church. He is the touch of God in every meeting, whatever the function on Church Life may be.

Kevin J. Conner
Melbourne, Australia
2015-16

About the Author

Born in Melbourne, Australia in 1927 and saved at the age of 14, Kevin Conner served the Lord in the Salvation Army until the age of 21. At this time he entered pastoral ministry for several years. After that, he was involved in teaching ministry in Australia, New Zealand and for many years at Bible Temple in Portland, Oregon. After serving as Senior Minister of Waverley Christian Fellowship for eight years (1987-1994), he continued to serve the church locally as well as ministering at various conferences and the continued writing of textbooks.

Kevin is recognised internationally as a teaching-apostle after his many years in both church and Bible College ministry. His textbooks have been used by ministers and students throughout the world. He has been in great demand as a teacher and has travelled extensively. Kevin passed away peacefully in Melbourne, Australia in February 2019 at the age of 92.

Visit Kevin's web site at <u>www.kevinconner.org</u> for more details about his life and ministry, as well as information about his 75+ books, his video courses, and his audio teaching podcast.

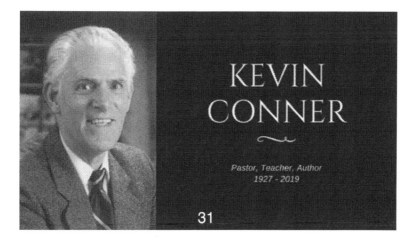

KEVIN
CONNER

Pastor, Teacher, Author
1927 - 2019

Kevin's Autobiography

Kevin Conner is known by many people around the world as a theologian, Bible teacher, and best-selling author of over 75 biblical textbooks. Although thousands of people have been impacted by his ministry and his writings, only a few people know his personal story. Kevin took the time to detail his own life journey, including lessons gleaned along the way, in his autobiography "This is My Story" back in 2007. It is now available in the following formats:

- PDF download - visit www.kevinconner.org/shop
- International paperback or eBook from Amazon.
- Australian paperback from WORD books (www.word.com.au).

Kevin was an orphan who never met his dad or mum. He grew up in boy's homes before coming to faith in Jesus Christ in the Salvation Army in his teenage years. From there, his life took many turns as he continued to pursue his faith in God and his understanding of the Scriptures and church life. Follow his journey and gain wisdom for your own life and ministry as you read his intriguing life-story.

Other Books by Kevin Conner

Acts, A Commentary
An Evaluation of Joseph Prince's Book 'Destined to Reign'
Are Women Elders Biblical?
Biblical Principles of Leadership
The Christian Millennium
1 & 2 Chronicles, a Commentary
1 Corinthians, a Commentary
The Church in the New Testament
The Church of the Firstborn and the Birthright
1 & 2 Chronicles, A Commentary
Colossians and Philemon, A Commentary
The Covenants (with Ken Malmin)
Daily Devotions (or Ministrations)
Daniel, An Exposition
The Day After the Sabbath
The Death-Resurrection Route
Deuteronomy, A Commentary
Esther, A Commentary
Exodus, A Commentary
Ezekiel, A Commentary
The Feasts of Israel
First Principles of the Doctrine of Christ
Foundations of Christian Doctrine
Foundations of Christian Doctrine (Self Study Guide)
Foundational Principles of Church Membership
Foundation Principles of the Doctrine of Christ
Frequently Asked Questions
Galatians, A Commentary
Genesis, A Commentary
Headship, Covering and Hats

Hebrews, A Commentary
The House of God
Interpreting the Book of Revelation
Interpreting the Scriptures (with Ken Malmin)
Interpreting the Scriptures (Self Study Guide)
Interpreting the Symbols and Types
Isaiah, A Commentary
James, A Commentary
Jeremiah and Lamentations, A Commentary
Joshua, A Commentary
Jude, A Commentary
Judges, A Commentary
Keep Yourself Pure
The Kingdom Cult of Self
Kings of the Kingdom - Character Studies on Israel's Kings
Law and Grace
Leviticus, A Commentary
The Lord Jesus Christ our Melchizedek Priest
Maintaining the Presence
Marriage, Divorce and Remarriage
Messages from Matthew
Methods and Principles of Bible Research
Ministries in the Cluster
The Ministry of Women
The Minor Prophets, A Commentary Mystery
Mystery Parables of the Kingdom
The Name of God
New Covenant Realities
New Testament Survey (with Ken Malmin)
Numbers, A Commentary
Old Testament Survey (with Ken Malmin)

Only for Catholics
Passion Week Chart
Philippians, A Commentary
Psalms, A Commentary
The Relevance of the Old Testament to a New Testament
Church Restoration Theology
Restoration Theology
Revelation, A Commentary
Romans, A Commentary
The Royal Seed
Ruth, A Commentary
1 & 2 Samuel, A Commentary
Sermon Outlines (3 volumes)
The Seventy Weeks Prophecy
Studies in the Royal Priesthood
The Sword and Consequences
The Tabernacle of David
The Tabernacle of Moses
The Temple of Solomon
Table Talks
Tale of Three Trees
1 & 2 Thessalonians, A Commentary
This is My Story (Kevin Conner's autobiography)
This We Believe
Three Days and Three Nights (with Chart)
Tithes and Offerings
Today's Prophets
To Drink or Not to Drink
To Smoke or Not to Smoke
Two Kings and a Prince
Understanding the New Birth and the Baptism of the Holy
Spirit

Vision of an Antioch Church
Water Baptism Thesis
What About Israel?

Visit www.kevinconner.org for more information.
Visit www.amazon.com/author/kevinjconner for a list of other books by Kevin Conner.

Video Training Seminars

Kevin Conner's popular "Key of Knowledge" Seminar is now available as an online teaching course. Part 1 covers 'Methods and Principles of Bible Research' and includes over 6 hours of video teaching, the required textbooks, extra hand out notes, and a self-guided online study program. The first lesson, 'Challenge to Study' is FREE.

The second part of Kevin Conner's "Key of Knowledge" Seminar is about 'Interpreting the Bible' and includes over 7 hours of video teaching, two downloadable textbooks, extra hand out notes, and a self-guided online study program. These two courses can be taken as stand-alone courses, in succession, or simultaneously.

Also available at www.kevinconner.org/courses is Kevin's extensive teaching on his best-selling book The Foundation of Christian Doctrine, which includes 67 videos which can be purchased in 4 parts.

Visit the courses page at www.kevinconner.org for all the details.

Kevin Conner's Audio Teaching

Dozens of Kevin Conner's messages are available on his FREE teaching podcast - 'Kevin Conner Teaches'. This podcast is accessible from Apple Podcasts, Google Podcasts, or Spotify Podcasts (if you are a subscriber), as well as at www.kevinconner.podbean.com (including on the Podbean mobile App).

New messages are published weekly, selected from messages Kevin has given over the years at various churches, conferences, and training seminars. Be sure to subscribe so you are notified of recent releases.

Visit https://www.kevinconner.org/audios-by-kevin/ for a full list of podcast titles and series.

PDF Versions of Kevin Conner's Books

All of Kevin Conner's books are now available to purchase in quality PDF format. This digital format is in addition to the Kindle eBooks and paperback/hardback versions currently available. A PDF is a 'portable document format' used on all computers for reading documents. Books in this format can be read on a computer, laptop, or handheld device and/or printed out for your personal use (even stored in your own binding of choice). Many PDF readers also allow you to 'mark-up' and add your own notes to the document. PDFs of Kevin's books are for your personal use and are not for copying or redistribution.

You can purchase PDF books at www.kevinconner.org/shop. Upon payment, a download link will be sent to you via email along with your receipt.

Resources by Mark Conner

Kevin Conner's son, Mark Conner, worked closely with him in the church ministry for many years (as music director and youth pastor), before succeeding him in 1995 as the Senior Minister of what was then Waverley Christian Fellowship (now CityLife Church) Mark transitioned out of that role in early 2017 and since that time has been giving himself to speaking, training, coaching, and writing.

Here is a list of Mark's books which may be of interest to you:

* *Transforming Your Church - Seven Strategic Shifts*
* *Money Talks: Practical Wisdom for Becoming Financially Free*
* *The Spiritual Journey: Understanding the Stages of Faith*
* *How to Avoid Burnout: Five Habits of Healthy Living*
* *Prison Break: Finding Personal Freedom*
* *Pass the Baton: Successful Leadership Transition*
* *Successful Christian Ministry*

These can be purchased from:
* Amazon.com/author/markconner in paperback and eBook format.
* WORD books in Australia (www.word.com.au)
* www.kevinconner.org/books-by-mark-conner/ in PDF format.

Mark also has an active BLOG and teaching podcast. Visit www.markconner.com.au for more information.

Made in the USA
Middletown, DE
23 September 2023

39155338R00026